last penny the sun

poems

Laura M Kaminski

Published by Balkan Press

ISBN 978-0-9914802-2-7

TABLE OF CONTENTS

Pistis

Penelope sits before her tapestry, weaves what she sees:
the coast below the cliff, the barren beach.

Her suitors empty their cups, swallow the final morsels
from their plates and lick their fingers.

They stand and shake their robes, call for torches
to light the path along the ledge that feeds the sea.

Their laughter, their amorous, arduous words
finally fade beneath the tide's murmuring breath.

Penelope exhales—she pulls a silver pin
from her hair, frees the waves to tumble;

she scratches another faint mark on the frame of the loom,
then uses the flattening silver point to loosen stitches,

making room within the threads to weave this scene again
tomorrow, perhaps be able to stitch a glimpse of sail.

Mary Martha

I wish I could cleave myself in two, split
my image cleanly, let my Mary sit and bathe your
feet, caress your ankles, stroke your hair, release
all her aspirations to provide, impress, prepare
into the kitchen—

where they will cluster around my Martha like
a twist of hungry cats, waiting to be placated
by her incessant motion. My Martha juggles
pot-holders with the efficiency of lactic acid—
a gesture of affection might burn rice.

But it was Martha, only Martha, who watched
for you to come home, a hopeful sentry
with a dish-damp towel in her hands.

Returning from Machu Picchu

for Bill and Diane Bottoms; italicized phrases are from Pablo Neruda's "Heights of Macchu Picchu" Cantos I, VI, VIII, X & XII in The Essential Neruda: Selected Poems, *Mark Eisner/City Light Books, 2004*

Mum said you are returning from Machu Picchu—
before I call you, I want to learn a little more
so I have a better understanding what this means—

I present myself before the bookcase Ouija, watch
my hand move over Grandpa's old blue atlas,
hover and change directions, descend and retrieve
The Essential Neruda: Selected Poems.

Empty streets, farmers' quarter—from there, did you
climb up, flower by flower, through the thicket,
each footfall-polished stone raising you higher
up the staircase of air until the void?
Did you stand *next to the feet of the eagle?*

Did the thin air sear your throat, language grow heavy,
imprisoned on your tongue *for a thousand years?*
Did your heart beat in your ears, erasing words?
Did it flutter in the cage of your body until you
released it to hover, weightless, between sky and earth?

Did you leave it *between the streets and the atmosphere*
when you *returned to the jasmine of the exhausted
human springtime?* I am ready now. Bring me
your story. *Tell me everything,*

stone upon stone.

It's a PIRATE!

A voice/ speaking in all languages announced that/ the End of Days was upon us,
divine wisdom/ would be granted to all mankind, and the secret/ of eternal peace
would be revealed./ It involves ice cream. —from William Bernhardt's poem
"What Happened While I Was Away?" in The White Bird, *Balkan Press, 2013*

The boy behind me at the grocery—all of five,
perhaps just a tall three—is standing by their basket
tightly clutching a huge yellow box of Cheerios.

He points at me, my face, the black glass lens
that covers my left eye. Despite his mother's
desperate shushing, he's audible four aisles over:

"It's a PIRATE!"

Other shoppers stop to peer around the corner—
at him, at me, his blushing mother—as if finally
they'll get to see the emperor without his clothes.

I excuse myself to the cashier waiting ready
for my money, hit the linoleum with my knees,
get right up in the young man's face and answer:

"ARRRGGHH!"

When my ship calls it a day and heads into
the harbor, when sails are furled and barnacles
scraped, when useful life is over, when I've

grown obsolete and friends gather to remember,
share stories, decommission me with honors,
I hope someone laughs and thinks to tell

how once I flew
the Jolly Roger.

Miss Caroline Pickersgill Remembers

for poet and historian Christopher T. George, based on a paragraph in his Terror on the Chesapeake: The War of 1812 on the Bay, *White Mane Books, 2000*

He called on mother—the Commodore brought with him
a Lieutenant Colonel and a General—Commodore Barney
came to call at our corner house on Pratt and Albemarle.

Major Armistead had said that they were ready at the Star Fort,
Fort McHenry, to repel the British, keep them from invading,
stand fast and stop the enemy—ready but for one thing:

Fort McHenry had no symbol to raise defiant, steadfast on
the flagpole, no ensign to hearten men and mark the ground
that they must hold. So the Commodore called on mother—

Missus Mary Pickersgill—to make an order (far bigger than
anyone before had ever made) for the largest flag a garrison
had ever raised. Four hundred yards of bunting plus

a little more for places that might need to be reinforced.
We had to go over to the brewery and use their floor to cut
and piece. My knees wore my skirts thin from crawling

up and down those wide stripes hemming—fifteen
of them—the bottom one was red and forty-two feet long.
I started stitching stripes while mother worked on stars—

straight lines are easier, piecing points is hard—stars each two
feet wide, fifteen of those, same as the stripes, in a huge sky
of blue. (I used to dream that I was pressing heaven's seams.)

We'd already heard more than plenty of the horrors of the war—
in every knot, I tied a prayer their soldiers wouldn't ravish
Baltimore. And we wore gloves while we were sewing so our

fingers wouldn't bleed into the bunting. When my hands were
too sore and tired for the needle, I stood by mother, pushed up her
spectacles...again and again and again...and trimmed the lamp.

But when it flew above the Fort that morning (after all-night
battle, rain and rockets, bombing), my eyes filled and heart swelled
near to bursting: I'd done my bit, me, Caroline, age thirteen.

Collage: Naturalizing Americans

with thanks to Mark Twain, and pages from Wireless *and* Gurney's *catalogs*

Famous figures bobble-heads—a nod to history, caricatures, 3D.
There's Lincoln in a great black hat, Mark Twain's in a captain's cap,
and Washington's bewigged. I dig for other pages, scraps,
among the final strips and bits of winter kindling;

the only picture-pages left are gardening. My eyes fall
on the "patio blueberry," shown in a ten-gallon pot, the perfect
size to paste atop the narrow furrowed brow of Mr. Lincoln—
and I'm off! Next, a branch of cherry, cut and trimmed;

I scatter blossoms among Washington's snowdrift curls.

Finally, in the crown of the steamboat hat I nest a great green
egg, Missouri Moon-and-Stars, a southern watermelon sweet enough
to leave Eve unrepentant. It looks heavy; I take a pencil,

sketch in an extra bit of straw for comfort,
make this country and its history my own.

My Grandfather's Parka

honoring the memory of Rev. W.R. Bottoms, Lt. Col. (Ret.), U.S. Army

I look at my husband at the edge
of the lake, bundled and warm,
in an inherited parka—
my grandfather's parka—
watching ripples of the molten
glacier greeting sunlight.

Some half a century ago and more,
this parka—
my grandfather's parka—
wrapped him, young and strong
and proud, a chaplain with
the U.S. Army in the alpine snows
of Europe, its holocaustic winter.
When we received it, the inside
pocket clutched and held protected
(against those years and that
excessive darkness) his worn
copy of a book of prayers,
Prayers for the Armed Forces,
prayers of comfort, prayers of
courage, prayers of kindness
for the enemy, and the words
to give before and after every, every
every time of dying.

How often, while the snows fell
on his hood and on his
shoulders, did his chapped
fingers, gloves removed to

offer a final human touch,
a steadying handhold to
the dying as they passed
on to meet with God—how
often did his fingers split
their cold-dried skin and
bleed (unnoticed) in the pockets
of my grandfather's parka?

We travelled in October, a late
vacation at the lake, but now
in these still waters I glimpse
a ripple of the truth: we
were only transportation for
the celestial gyroscope, our
journey was not, as we thought,
about us. We really only came
to bring the parka—
my grandfather's parka—
to quietly sway with the
small morning waves. We are
only one small eddy in the
universal balance, rocking gently.
We only came to bring his parka
to a place of peace.

Explication

response to a lesson from Mike Dockins regarding a one-line poem by Franz Wright called "The Forties"

I wrote until the page became a hundred thousand paper cranes.

Slow-Winning: Peace Lesson from Smith and White

after poems "Lilting" by R.T. Smith and "Napalm Girl" by Patti White, both
appearing in the Atlanta Review's anthology The Gift of Experience, *2005*

Peace is slow-winning—
the lilting song of the Irish widow
rises through the roof-beams,
through the chimney of the pub and curls
into smoke-wisps gathering
beneath a heavy, low ceiling of clouds,
her song a wordless flute-less flighted
thing no law can bar and cage.
Peace is slow-winning—
it is the chubby smiling
grandchild of a girl who
once we all saw in a photo,
napalm-flaming, naked, screaming—
she survived, she married,
her grandson spoons cold ravioli
from a can into a bowl—
when one slips from the spoon and
falls on the floor with a splat, he laughs
and she does not correct him.

War-Torn

for Sean Dustman, USN; book ref. JRR Tolkien

Draped in a shawl, dusty and torn
Her body curled impossibly small
Into the concrete corner shadow of the shelter—
A bit of debris dropped from the bottom of a spider's web—
The ship's kitten, immobilized by exhaustion and terror,
Shoved damp and hurried by an old, rough hand
Into the bottom of that last wooden lifeboat—

Perhaps not debris, not a kitten
But surely too completely still to be a girl—

Herself curled impossibly small
Into the concrete corner shadow of her mind—
Looking out
Looking in—
She's back at that other time
Before the mechanical predators' roar
Back when she gathered rocks at the bed of the river,
Thrilling at how some catch her eye in sun,
Others in shade—

But even here she is not free
Even here along the river's bed she sees
Instead of trees
Green-clad soldiers growing straight and tall
Along the banks between the river
And the road.

* * *

They laugh at themselves,
At each other,
At the tinny techno-pop playing
From a tiny radio with a blown speaker—

They laugh at each other's attempts to translate
Station-breaks and advertisements
Delivered in a language they only partly understand—
They laugh and compose messages aloud
That they'd like to deliver to their families—

They laugh and remember and try to calculate
Which one of them has gone the longest
Since reaching a hand into a cooler
Filled with ice-cubes and half-frozen beers.

They are not children—
Their laughter isn't cruel—
They are all graduates with honors
From the fantasy of an "adventure job."
The laughter is a river of common ground,
A perseverance flowing over and around
The undercurrent and obstacles
Of things that can't be said.
The river keeps moving and doesn't ask questions.

They do not speak of the girl—
Without speaking, they already know
Tomorrow they will take her with them,
Take turns carrying her and squeezing water
From a canteen-dampened rag into her mouth.

They do not speak of the girl—
They will not turn their calculations
From ice and beer
To how much it will slow them—
How much risk moving slower will add.

They do not speak of it—
Tomorrow they will carry her,
And the next day, and perhaps another—
Until they join up with another unit—
Some unit that, perhaps, still has its medic.

* * *

Tomorrow the trees in her forest
Will lift her into their gnarled arms
And carry her away
Like those giant, mythical creatures
From that book she's never read.

Before the Priest

Before the priest comes up to pack your last
remaining sins, cinch them with a blessing,
discard them with the rest of your hazardous
waste and personal effects—

give me a moment now
before you swallow your last
moments, gulp that absolution,
let them wrap you in that shroud—

I'm not here to rally or campaign
or bring you comfort, not even cheer
or cheer you on as you dress down
to your raw, immortal soul—

I'm here only to ask you
while you're winding down the hours
have you had the chance to do
all your forgiving?

If not, then I'll kneel
and pray for more time.

Meditatio Divina

after "Lectio Divina" by Kate Fadick, from the Tupelo Press 30/30 Project, December 2013

some words spark, hot flares
seeking tinder, hungry
to ignite, consume

they fly free during
the act of sharpening
edges of old swords

fall into pockets
set fire to gathered lint
we had forgotten

suddenly angry,
we radiate this heat
begin to shoot flames

burning, fall victim
to whims of every breeze,
uncontrolled, carried—

how to make ploughshares
without creating shards
that set off new wars—

if we knew, would not
our fields already be
turned and tilled, our hands

caked with loamy soil,
us already shoulder
to shoulder planting?

Fable One: Separation

this series of ten "Fables" is dedicated to Jeannine Burton

The climbing rose, much-loved with blossoms of many
colors, Joseph's Coat, took a strange step, a leap

off some evolutionary cliff. Each blossom-bearing
stem began to show a pinch, as if some invisible

tourniquet was tightening, each stem a long green
earthworm now dividing. And every rose, red

or gold or peach or something blended in between
was pinched off into alonedom—each grew its own

toes, small new feet, stepped down, began to wander.
Some were excited, some uncertain, slower.

After only twenty minutes the novelty wore thin, toes grew
tired of the unfamiliar and each of these strange creatures

sought a place to stop for rest and reassurance, a place
to feel comfortable again, fit in. They flocked like birds—

all the mostly-yellows grouped under the tomatoes, reds
gathered by the potting shed, oranges, peaches, splashed

or specked—all gathered into their small sets with those
that looked most like them, a scurrying, divisive migration.

No scissors needed now when you step out to gather
flowers for the table; they are not connected to their roots,

might even voice objections if your bouquet-collection
deigns to use stems from other color-coalitions, goes

full-spectrum, representation, comprehension. They are not
connected to their roots, some might even spit pollen

if you mention that, to you, the variation in their hues
makes them, in combination in a vase, more beautiful—

if you mention you suspect them of having common
origins, if you dare say they all smell the same.

Fable Two: Climbing

I'd been distressed as I perused
your straight-line plan

to climb a mountain high as
Everest. Such an ascent takes
time, is perhaps best tackled
in large looping circles.

True, circumambulation comes
with its own frustrations—
progress seems so slow when
you look down below you

on the slope and spy your own
old notes of bright ambition,
words you wrote eight months ago
that you'd now prefer to hide.

And it's also true we do grow
older on the way, the air gets
thinner, colder, and some days
we struggle to remember

why we came, fight to fill our lungs
and hearts, inhale life and one more
time distill its beauty, exhale
one more phrase.

Still. Keep. Moving. Slowly.
Upward.

Fable Three: Pausing

We continue upward, approach another
bend. Here, the air is fragrant, sweetened
by the blossoms of a wild rose that's found
a crevice in the cliff, taken root and grown.

Suddenly our own journey does not seem so
impossible. We pause here to rest, to savor.

We are not even asked here to remove
our shoes, not tasked with inscribing new
commandments. All we are called upon
to do is pause a moment, feel gratitude.

Fable Four: Rooting and Rotting

First, you must be stripped down—
remove not just your thorns, but blossom

too, and half your skin, surrender
to the guillotine and flaying. Stripped

of individuality and protection, you'll be left
alone in meditation, left to stand immersed

in liquid, nondescript and mostly naked
twig, standing in a clear jar in the window.

From here, there are only two
directions you can go—either begin

to grow fine threads to drink more
deeply, or refuse, choose instead

a wet rotting from the outside in
until you're taken out and added

to the compost. There isn't even
judgment of your preference—

either way, you'll still be useful
in the garden.

Fable Five: Immersion

regarding The Drowned Book: Ecstatic and Earthy Reflections of Bahauddin, the Father of Rumi, *translated by Coleman Barks & John Moyne, Harper One, 2004*

Two men sat
by a bubbling fountain—
Rumi and Shams—
Shams sat with his arms open;
Rumi's were tucked in.

The hands of Jellaludin
Rumi, son, were tightly
curled, clutched a notebook,
his father Bahauddin's
journal of reflections,
words of wisdom
and instruction.

And this carefully written
notebook was the topic
of the conversation Rumi
was having with his friend.

Rumi insisted he needed
these recorded musings
from his father.

Shams told him he
shouldn't cling so tightly
to the ink-blots of another.

Finally Shams grabbed and threw
the treasure in the fountain—

Rumi was left in shock,
an emptiness of breath and hands.

Before Rumi could speak again,
Shams told him: Not to worry—

it is only water—if you truly
need this booklet it will still be
fine after a brief immersion.

Reach in! Retrieve it!
Now we'll see if
Bahauddin's old inscriptions
are important.

The fountain wall on which they sat
has crumbled into rubble, seven
centuries and more of feet and wind
have turned its masonry to sand—

but *The Drowned Book*, those ancient
pages that were soaked, then saved—
remain available today, in English
translation even, and in print.

Fable Six: Dance

The dervishes are blown across
the desert lands like seeds,
they gather at the shrines
of Sufi saints to dance and pray,
they spin with arms stretched
up toward heaven, sprouting,
reaching for the light, longing
to learn to photosynthesize.

Fable Seven: Destruction

regarding the death of an oak in Syria, November 2013

Some call our dancing
heresy, took the shrine
at Atme, with their rifles
turned back those of us
who came to pray.

We gathered, then, within
the nearby shade of a large
weathered tree, made
our ablutions, spread our
carpets on the sand.

They came with axes,
proclaimed jihad with
chainsaws, toppled
the hundred-fifty-
year-old oak tree.

We take our mats—
the world is filled
with other places
to face the *qibla*.

Before we leave, we
turn and greet the angry
soldiers: Peace.

Fable Eight: Grafting

after instructions in The Drowned Book: Ecstatic and Earthy Reflections of Bahauddin, the Father of Rumi, *translated by Coleman Barks & John Moyne, Harper One, 2004*

Patience. Sunlight has travelled
eight minutes through the emptiness
to get here, gently warm the water
in the jar where this beheaded
rose-stem waits in suspended
animation. It does not show signs
of life, but neither has it rotted.

Patience. We have time. We might
as well read these old instructions,
maybe draw ourselves a diagram.
And see, there is a poplar growing
outside near the garden—look
through the window, you can see
from here—we will use that one.

Mise en place—we have assembled
our ingredients for this experiment:
one white poplar, one rose stem,
one long thin strip of woven linen.
There's one more, but it won't be
a problem—the soil here is sandy
clay and it just rained yesterday,
I can scoop a double-handful
of thick mud on the way if you'll
carry rose-stem jar and scalpel.

My hands are gooey, you make
the incision in the poplar—not
so high there, remember, I am
shorter than you are, please make
a cut that's low enough for me
to reach—peel back a patch
of bark and carve a tiny trough
as if you're making a coffin,
special-order, just to fit this stem.

When you're done stripping, take
the stem and coat it in this clay
that's in my hands, gently tuck
it in that crease to sleep, bind
the bark back over with the linen,
give it a good thick muddy blanket,
fill in the little grave, then I'll wipe
the surface smooth and let it dry.

And then we wait. More patience.
Enough we've time to ponder
the workings of the universe that
choose to save—this page in particular—
from destruction in that ancient fountain,
these instructions for *grafting*
the red rose to the white poplar.

Fable Nine: Gathering

The sapsucker-woodpecker, first
to return in spring, drills a ring
of taps right here and other
migratory birds, tired from their
travels, gather to renew their
strength. Even the hummingbird
comes to drink from this slow
fountain while she waits
for the approaching season
to arrive, to wake, to blossom.

Fable Ten/The End: Greeting

For years I've lived in isolation—
now strangers stop their cars
and walk across my yard in awe,
drawn to the rose now blooming
from the trunk of the white poplar.

I sit in the green fountain sprays
of its cascading stems, its blossoms.
Two petals fall and settle on the open
pages of my book. Another car
has stopped. I close the book and rise
to welcome guests. They are strangers.
Perfect strangers.

Joining the Lotus-Eaters

after Ayla Yeargain's "Intoxicating and Sweet"

Magnolia blossom—
someone squeezed
fresh lemon on a rose—
I had no hope
for unity
until just now.

Honeysuckle breathing
as the sun goes down—
I had not realized
how joy
persists
through darkness.

Night-blooming jasmine
laces the cup of the moon.
Ghost,
I know your secret,
know why
you couldn't leave.

Watermelon Vine

in memory of my father, Jerrell H Mathison

I planted watermelons in the garden
along the path where once my father
walked, content and curious, sampling
the growing greens and spicy peppers.

Now vines trail through every patch
and plot, touch fence-wires, investigate
tomatoes, marigolds, green onions, extend
tendrils, browsing as they journey.

In the morning mist, the wide leaves
stretch like fingered hands, palms cupped
to catch the raindrops. Blossoms take
their colors straight from the inks of dawn.

I sit among them holding up the last unplanted seed,
shiny black and oval, try to see in it the stencil
for the vine, try to see in the daughter
something patterned like the father.

Tea with Josiah II

after a Josiah Wedgwood and Sons tea service, c.1815-1820, in the Hill-Stead Museum collection in Farmington, CT.

Fire and pigment, mud and paste and glaze,
Josiah, you, like your father, knew the perfect
temperature required, and in those early days
while your daughter Emma played Chopin,
you found and tried and fired other clays:

You paid William Blake to illustrate
your catalogs, set an annuity for Samuel
Taylor Coleridge to focus on his poetry,
and like your father, spoke against
all slavery, called every man your brother.

And was it not in your parlor, over tea
that you convinced the Darwin family
to let your daughter's husband, Charles,
accept the offer of a berth upon the Beagle
to further his studies of botany?

You spent life giving fragile moments
form and permanence—fire and pigment,
clays and paste and glaze—and at the perfect
temperature, even after centuries,
these branches blossom.

Hand-Delivered

after "..pigtails" by Spiros Zafiris

at dawn,
I open your letter—
a flower
you forgot to leave
in my hair

Almost Seven

for Sean and Heather Dustman

She is "almost seven"—a designation
she insists on—she's sure she's outgrown
"six" now that she's moved beyond

those Chunky Coloring Stix to a full set
of hues tiered in their box-of-64 display.
She keeps her crayons sharpened.

She's made a map, a landscape-plat—
I can identify the oval of the driveway
clasped with a triangle (that means "house")

at the top of a lump of hill—a whole
page filled with bright waxes layered
heavily in patches like a quilt.

She explains: "Those are the color-vats
below the dirt—it's accurate, I did
research! You see the yellow circle?

That's the spot (she lisps) where the forsythia
sucks up color from a pond that's under,
and also all those daffodils that grow

between its toes. And here—you see
the polka-dots? Those are pots of paint
waiting for bluebonnets and dandelions

to drink them." I'm left speechless at this
gift, the insight of her "almost seventh" sense
and plant a kiss upon her tiny, busy forehead.

January snow. I am alone. I pull on boots
and carefully unfold my treasure map, slow-
slog over to the center of a snowdrift,

sink my soles in a deep pool of purple
banked with indigo—this is where
the irises will grow. Amid this blizzard-

swirling, it's good to have a way
to get my bearings, mix deductive
reckoning with hope, a diagram to find

and chart position when I'm snow-blind,
drop heart's anchor, hold me fast here
less than two feet off the rainbow.

Catechism

When still a small and prissy girl,
more prone
to matching bows and shoes
than digging inquisitive
holes in the mud,
it seemed clear that earthworms
fell from the clouds
with the rainwater.

I assumed those squirming
pink and brown segments were bits
of angels' intestines,
angels who'd met with mishaps,
buffeted to pieces
by the wind
or sliced by lightning.

Careful not to get anything
sacred on my socks, I tiptoed
through the debris,
sanctifying my squeamishness
with conviction.

Pas de Deux - Choreographed by Clark's Grebes

for Ream and Jennifer Stokley

entrée
Another year within
the wedding ring, I spin it on
my finger, contemplate

adagio
the blessing of a lifetime
mate, the delicate ballet, how
every *pas de deux* has a flyer

and a base, and how each year
our vows renew—you're still
for me, I'm still for you—

variations
and the most delightful
sight on this whole planet is
the mirror-dance of grebes—

each year, another *pas de deux*
upon the lake, by turns
imitate and lead, celebrate

each anniversary with
a display of grace—
despite webbed feet, they dance

their grand finale up
en pointe, beat their wings
as if in flight, meet each

other's eyes, their bodies
rise just above the surface
of the lake, their twin

hearts lift them up,
their love
walks on water—

coda
another year within the delicate
ballet, the blessing of a lifetime
mate, the wedding ring—

I spin it on my finger,
contemplate.

The Too-Close Shave

for my husband Kevin

I am looking at you while you shave
through a brushy decade's growth
of beard—first you used shears,
then the clippers from the tack-
room made for trimming mane
and tail. I watch, fascinated, as
the overgrowth departs in
layers, leaving only the
underbrush, the latest
iteration. I wonder (to
myself) how far you'll go,
when you will stop—
will you rip it all out,
scrape it with a heavy blade,
road equipment clearing
right down to the grade?
I watch you through the
bathroom door, and overcome
by metaphor, I slip, I
speak, I say "I hope you'll
keep the nose…" You say:

"You mean the mustache? Keep
the mustache?"

"No, the nose—I like the
natural features—I hope
you don't bulldoze the
eyes and nose…"

"Weirdo." You shut the door,
adjust your personal landscape
without inviting further
comments from the
neighborhood. I go outside,
look up at the moon.

I cannot see the man in it.
I know what happened.

Affectionately Yours (Ghazal)

writing as Halima bint Ayuba

It's claimed that the heart is the place of affection,
And yet some seem so hard, no trace of affection.

Divorce rates today almost match the marriages;
So hard to keep up with the pace of affection.

Some refuse to show heart, they cover their shoulders.
Some wear but the negligee lace of affection.

In the barnyard the startled pullets are fleeing,
The rooster pursues them in chase of affection.

A round woman waits—to see her obstetrician:
She has, clearly, another case of affection.

I am fond of the dog, she's fond of her dinner.
We meet at her food bowl, the base of affection.

Some poets write sonnets, they even say "love," but
Halima is hidden, an ace of affection.

Dark Slant (Ghazal)

writing as Halima bint Ayuba

Potatoes and secrets can keep in the dark
But eventually rot and leak in the dark.

Chickens are raucous and cackle in daylight
But they make not even a peep in the dark.

A coyote's howl gets the dog up for work
Patrolling, protecting the sheep in the dark.

The Loch Ness Monster has never been captured—
Does she still swim silently deep in the dark?

Long courtships give warnings of character flaws
But a one night stand is a leap in the dark.

A spotlighting poacher knows deer must come drink;
He waits with a gun by the creek in the dark.

Earth's gravity tugs on a meteor cloud;
When one falls, it makes a bright streak in the dark.

Some poets are wakeful and write all night long
Halima is lazy, asleep in the dark.

Traces, Odors, Signs

after Dan Veach's "Ancient of Days" in his book Elephant Water, *Finishing Line Press, 2012—with thanks for allowing his possums to wander*

Walking with the dog, we find
a bent, half-buried old road sign:
IRON COUNTY 118, block-lettered
in bas relief, and rusted.

I read with eyes and mind; that's all
it says to me. But the dog—she reads
with her whole body, leans forward,
quivers, points and sniffs and sits.
She stands again and licks it—tastes
the traces, odors, signs; inhales entire
histories into her eager mind.

She smells the nudging of a deer. Perhaps
a rabbit sat right here, small birds danced
in a puddle in the dent—maybe a family
of possums walked across, nose to tail
in a strange, swaying line.

After a while, she grasps the upturned corner
in her jaws, paws it loose and turns it over.

And suddenly, I'm on my knees
and begging, longing for this literacy—
"Teach me!
I did not know
there was another
page."

Creek-Fishing

the fisherman is painted into the creek
in shades of mist by a cloudy morning

his heart beats beneath the clear
reflective surface of the water
propelled by the undulation of spine
course checked by fin-veils, angling

slow curiosity sliding against the current
vacant hunger agape and waiting
where the artery, underwater, branches

his line can stand the test—a filament
stretching strong across this distance—
he catches himself, reels in, puts up
a fight, is silent-patient through the struggle

at the end, there is no net: his heart swings
free into his wet, waiting hands—gently,
gently, he removes the hook

Disability and Dog

She is impatient
while I try to smell
the wild news
the savory stew of air
in that top inch
above the ground
when the soil is damp
the leaves are last
year's leftovers
the grass decayed—

me with such a tiny
nose so poorly
placed high off
the ground I have no
real hope of pulling out
just one thread from
this tangle, just one
odor to yelp about
and wag and follow
just one piece of history
written in the olfactory—

I cannot follow the trail.

She pities me
sorry to leave me
behind and ignorant
while molecules slip
easily, urgently

into her nose—
sorry to leave me
behind but she
has got to go—

she's onto something.

Ogham: How the Rain Writes 'Forever'

Rivulets run through letters of an ancient alphabet—
chisel-cut angles form words along edges of gray
granite. The water reads, and then erodes the message,
travels deeper, ocean-bound along the aquifer.

Water returns, always, in another incarnation—
today, against a slate-gray sky, it comes again as rain.

It falls in shifting angles, writing letters, writing words,
hesitates, then writes again, recalling what it learned
back when, back on another continent while kissing
stone. I step into the ancient script and stand here,
soaking, trying to catch with reverent hands
wet whispers, trying to trace angles of the rain.

The Birthplace of Sturgeon

The current iterations of these ancients
mature as slowly as their ancestors, wait
two decades, often more, before they're
sure this is a world fit for roe.

Each year they slide with argyle sides
through seasons, summer winter lurk
in dim-lit murk at the bottom of the lake
and wait, trace the riverbed up to the dam.

They have no draw toward the hatchery,
so they investigate the boundaries, underwater
edges of the basin, around and again and return,
around and again and return until the storm.

It floods and weakens shorelines, splits a fissure
in a dam that they can reach—and suddenly, they've
gone glacier-ward to spawn, to a home they've never
known but through the writing in their bones.

Capacity

Exhausted blood flows into the heart, depleted.
The heart embraces it, gives it a squeeze,
sends it off again, rejuvenated.

In the wide embrace of morning, my heart
seems too small, this water-skin of self
that it maintains quite insignificant.

With my sensations I take in so much, hear
and see and smell and taste and touch
a world that's becoming tired, stale.

I want to expand my heart, become a heart
that beats with each thing I take in,
refreshes and invigorates sights,

sensations, situations, gives everything a scrub
and hug, reassuring and releasing all things
back to their courses, emptying

completely, keeping nothing for myself
except capacity.

Security

What if the sun was picky
with its gravity? What if
it could choose what it
permitted in its orbits,
what things it swallows
up and burns, what
it lets sweep past, untouched,
a comet that never
makes another pass?

I count on the unconditional
attraction daily, the security
of the gravitational embrace—
call it a faith in mercy, faith
so confident it doesn't even
own a mirror, has no churning
doubts to check, no vanity
and no regrets.

Version

for Christopher J Johnson

I love this English language
with its intrinsic recognition
of our need for rhythm
to syncopate our blues

permission to reVerse
our attitudes, share
a conVersation,
create a celebration
of diVersity

(you sound like you, I sound like me)

our words raindrops
each Versio phrase
making its solitary way
to the ocean where they
meet and greet each other

(all stop: watch the sound-waves)

I love this language English
with its intrinsic recognition
that the unfolding uniVerse
is all one poem.

Classical Education: Elizabethan Drama

poem ending with a line from Shakespeare

It is almost dark. I have a flashlight
in my hand, not yet switched on. I'm
looking for the dog. I find her flat
upon her belly, hidden in the grass;
between her paws she's grasped
a marmot skull, long since bleached
white, picked clean of flesh. I shine
the beam onto the luminescent
face of bone that faces hers. She
has conducted her examination with
her tongue—the skull is glossy wet.
She looks up at me, a telepathic moment:
I knew him well, Horatio.

Weeping Birch

after excerpt from "Travelogue—Short Stories" by Kathryn Gessner in
Illuminations: Expressions of the Personal Spiritual Experience *edited by Mark L.*
Tompkins and Jennifer McMahon, Celestial Arts, 2006

In Chico, California a weeping birch
reaches long root arms deep
into the past to welcome
a memory: a day when she
was freed from the brittle, cracking
black shell of a nursery-pot,
given a place and a purpose.
Her roots were barely fingers then,
wrapped like a shroud about
the still-feathered recent body
of an owl that left its shell
upon a traveler's windshield,
traded up for more permanent
wings. The birch reaches deep.
The owl returns as a poem,
a jewel in a blossom, a blue
whisper extracted from moonlight.

Call It a Win

for Bob Rhodes, to put a face on the faceless; after the marble "Nike of Samothrace"-- also known as the "Winged Victory"-- circa 190 BC, at the Louvre in Paris; and in honor of a caregiver I've met only by phone, Ms. Dawn; when I asked if she was still reading poetry to a deteriorating friend, she answered "Sure, I'm here to do what they can't do for themselves—got to keep feeding him poems. I think he likes the short ones better now."

Before we have to cut
the harp-strings here,
dear Listener, I'd like
to try to paint your picture,
try with words instead
of colors. I'll use a model
made of marble who lives
at the Louvre in Paris.

Twenty-two centuries old,
yet she still holds her pose
on the prow of a broken ship.
Like you, she is faceless,
and her arms are missing
but what is left depicts you
perfectly, hints at your secret:

time may damage and erode
limbs of flesh as well as
marble, limit your reach,
how far you can extend, take
and break your eyes and hands
until you can no longer
even see the words or turn
the page without assistance—

but as long as you can listen
when someone reads aloud,
you too stand undefeated
on the prow, facing ever
forward, homeward bound

and soaring, redefining
"Victory" as this: you still
have wings. And each
poem you hear is a feather,
each poem a little feather.

Hush

for Mike Dockins, after Dario Robleto's conceptual art sculpture "Lunge For Love As If It Were Air" in his 2012 exhibition "The Prelives of the Blues" at the New Orleans Museum of Art—labeled "stretched audiotape of two now-deceased lovers' recordings of each other's heartbeats"

They recorded each other's
beating hearts—rewind, imagine
for a moment, each one's hand
holding the small voice-recorder
to the surface of the other's
naked chest, the careful capture
of the rhythmic flutter trapped
within the skin-draped arc-
bars of the ribcage.

Leases finished on
flesh accommodations, they
moved out, left only
recorded lengths of audiotape
now stretched and shaped into two
feathers placed together
in a large glass mason jar.

Here our poem must enter
reverently, remove its shoes.
No need to speak further—
listen. Let your own heart
be God's ear.

Scoring the Music

in memory of Jack Hutton, an extraordinary musical soul

In the measure between dawn's unlit stretch
and morning, he sits motionless

He is listening, hands unmoving, knows
his grasp is yet imperfect

But he is learning to hear it all—
the woodpeckers' drums, the squirrels' castanets

The stringed hum of each wing-beat
the voice of every bird

He knows when he can hear it, he can
score it, every breath and tap and warble

And it will be the fingerprint of God—
ink everywhere.

Ways with Grapes

The grapes are growing, blushing
darker on the vine, rich juice
and dusky husk combined, as if
a heaven made of honey rained,
and these are dew. To those
who compose music, they are wine,
fermented, aged, notes and tones
and characters, the compositions
then distilled, refined into a brandy,
set aflame.

Poems are made from these same grapes,
these same fine drops of nectar—
left in sunlight, these droplets
evaporate and dry. Waiting and sunlight
make a poem, a song that can
be held between the fingers,
arias and cantatas dried
to lunch-box- and pocket-size,
a symphony in a handful,
come-as-you-are, take-along heaven
common raisin.

Raisins

The cathedral bell-wall stands patiently in the sun
like a street-performer waiting for a space
before beginning his act again,
taking a rest, then starting over.

The crowds gather, any real curiosity
about history sapped by the heat,
leaching out of them in damp patches
forming under the armpits of their
short-sleeved shirts.

They aim their cameras on autopilot,
they must bring home the obligatory photo;
this cathedral
is the one
on all the postcards from this place.

They will appreciate it more in a week or two,
viewed two-dimensionally in air-conditioning.
They will look at it with awe and think
how much they must have enjoyed it.

They will try to recall, precisely,
the cacophonic spell
cast beneath the noonday sun
by the pealing of the bells.

They will try to sift
the iron harmonies
out of the heat-deafness

caused by beads of sweat
forming on the scalp and forehead.

They will sift and stir
and knead and shape
a flat tortilla of memory
baked in the heat.

They will hang it
on the walls of their minds
and touch it fondly
with fingers of thought
in the winter.

In another two decades,
or three,
they will finally
remember
the sound of the bells,
the priest at the ropes
at the base
of the bell-wall
reaching and pulling
each in turn,
coaxing notes of sweet
endurance
into the deafening
call to mass.

Small against the wall's
magnificence,

he is sweat-rumpled
and serene,

a raisin of holiness
sustained
by a host
of white tortillas
and a chalice
of warm communion
wine.

Mad Hatter

after Lewis Carroll's wonderful characters

The Mad Hatter and March Hare
Invited us to tea
They couldn't interest Alice
But they captivated me

They're arguing and irritating
(Put on my sleeping cap)
Debating and deliriating
(I have a little nap)

They are truly rotten hosts
Although they do their best
It's why I love when they invite me
Because I'm a rotten guest

They yell and pound the table
They scream, they shout, they pout
I'm ignoring and I'm snoring
And my tongue is hanging out

Alice prefers the angels
Who are patient and polite
But there's very little I can learn
From beings who are always right

It doesn't interest me as much—
That "created holiness"—
As the holy fragments to be found
In the rest of us under the mess

Angels are bright and shiny,
Reliable, accurate, true—
But God created man from mud
And as we muddle through

The very best that I can offer
(Blackened kettle to blackened pot)
Is to be alert when you are shining
And be snoring when you're not.

Complaint

I hate the mornings-in-a-hurry—
I tend to worry
whether I'll have time to get
the breakfast dishes done.

So while I'm cooking, my mind
does not stand with me—it's
displaced, already at the sink
and sudsing, washing up.

I hate the mornings-in-a-hurry—
by the time I've finished eating
I've already had to scrub
the skillet twice.

Karma

A chipped enamel bowl
painted with a blue rose
holds the damp pit of
a single ripe plum

The knife is balanced carefully
between bowl and table
still nectar-slick

A bee lands on this gangplank
begins to sip its way
to blissful lethargy

Not until the afternoon shadows
become dark and long
does it emerge from trance

And practices three times
its navigational dance
before it returns to perform

At the hive.

After watching the complexities
of its gyrations,
its tiny marches,
its abdomen pointing down,
its boogie and its shimmy—
then its gossamer of wings
and gone

After watching,
tomorrow you know
they will come
to this shrine.

Tomorrow morning, will you
slice another plum,
and leave it
moist and dripping,
uneaten
on the patio table

While from inside
you watch
their wet feasting

And gratefully sip
your hot orange tea
with honey?

Instinct

after Allen M Weber's "The Wintering Bee"

Vibrant winged voices of clover
and briar-rose hum an innuendo
through the sultry air of summer.

Is it some deeper instinct now
that makes us crave the granular nectar
of watermelon crushed in the mouth,
tangy translucence of lemonade
in a glass of melting ice cubes,
a pollen-dusting of sugar
around the rim?

Angel of the Composite Photograph

for my mother, Joyce B Mathison

In the dry creek bed, he is the trickle
of faithful water that flows
under the soil's dusty surface.

Beneath the overpass, he is the wisp
of sprayed graffiti that's stretched beyond
the bubbled names to form an owl.

On the certificate you've dressed up to accept
he's one small swirl, ornately
invisible, hidden in the script.

Above you, deep in the cobwebbed barn
he is the heavy nail, rusted, bent
obscured by shadow, holding together nothing.

You'll never see him wearing wings—unless somehow
you spy the shimmering fly that's sitting
under the table, perfectly still and silent.

He is the unseen spectator, present
in every congregation. He is a single straw
in the leaky thatched roof of your heart.

He doesn't miss a moment. His memory
is photographic. He always catches you from the perfect
angle, at your finest—he's taking snapshots, making

a collage, choosing carefully, showing only your
best side in one composite picture he affixes
to your passport for your journey to meet God.

Offering

after "Themeless" by Mike Dockins, Tupelo Press 30/30 Project, January 2014

I remember spring, when hope
could not contain itself, burst in
the rush of daffodils trying to grow
tall enough to blossom.

I remember summer confidence,
fruit set well on the apple, poplar
saplings doubled their height.

In autumn, I wanted to catch a pair
of fireflies in a jar, and save them
for later like I did the pumpkins,
but even I knew their light could not
last through the winter.

I have harvested such abundance
from those few seeds I scattered
that I want to share. I check in
the freezer, wish that I had found
a way to put up that falling meteor,
the shooting star I tied a wish
on back in August.

No fireflies, no shooting star—
you need a comet, and I don't
even have a moth to offer.

All I've got left in my freezer
are green peppers—though

if you'd like, I'd gladly send you
some of those.

Facing the Wall

for Brian Sanders

I stand outside
in chill November moonlight—
I face the wall.
I want to paint my shadow here,
how the shoulder of my coat
bunches up toward upturned collar,
how a wisp of hair escapes, delighted,
from my hood.
I face the wall—
I step in toward it and I see
the enlarging patch of darkness
grow to meet me till I'm swallowing
myself, am almost self-absorbed.
I face the wall—
step back and notice how
I'm becoming small, smaller with
each backward step I take into
the source of light.
I want to paint my shadow here,
no larger than a thumb-print,
no darker than invisible—
I face the wall.

The Year in Summary

for Laurie Byro, after "Questions About Angels" by Billy Collins

At market we stop to drink
tea with the fortune-teller—

it's been an off year; she gives us
half-cups of "Great Value."

At home, we try to change our fate,
steep a glass pot of Earl Grey.

We bought her grey parrot,
we've named it Ezekiel—

it's learning to say:
"These bones can live."

Our cellar hides a bottled garden,
jar after jar with ghosts of poems in them.

"Billy Collins" says this label. "One angel
on a pin-head." She's still dancing.

Waypoint

for Laura Bottoms, after the traditional carol "The Twelve Days of Christmas"

Last night we passed
the waypoint once again,
the place we mark the years
as "ends" "begins"

and our round raft sets another
looping autopilot course
in this ocean without a shore,
this universe.

I wake at dawn on
January one, set out
the door for the horizon,
take the long walk

in peach-frosted light
my heart beats residual carols
in a sustained vibrato,
insists on celebrating

all twelve days. So be it.
This morning I walk
to the edge of the raft,
look over in time to catch

the space in space where
the last day of the old year
has left a trace of ripples,
a wake in this dark liquid

as a bevy of seven
black-ruffled swans moves away.
And tonight, I'll scan our local
galaxy for milking-maids.

Catching the Eye of al-Samakah

after Abayomi Animashaun's "Playing Tennis with the Net Down" in his book The Giving of Pears, *Black Lawrence Press, 2010*

Abayo, my friend, let me borrow your net—
there is a fish I need to catch
to make a coat to keep me warm
before the winter weather comes.

Fish, lend me your fire-opal eye,
I'm sewing a new coat cut from sky,
embroidering star-signs on its yoke
where Gemini will guard my throat

from my collar block each shiver,
while the Archer on my shoulder from his quiver
sends arrows from a yew-bow strung with light
to disappear beyond the hem of night.

Aquarius pours rivulets down my wrists—
Fish, lend me your eyes to button this
cuff into a circle that can hold
the shimmering members of the Pisces shoal.

When I pull you from Abayo's net,
do not veer leaping from my grasp,
no struggles to break clear, no
fear, no need to even gasp—

when I've caught you, al-Samakah,
for the glowing eye you'll lend me
I'll release you to swim with your starlit kin
upon my sleeve's infinity.

Whirling

for Daniel Wasserman

The stars become drowsy
watching me—
The cosmos has classed me
as an amateur performer.

Planets and comets alike
turn their attentions
to the professionals—
they will stay awake all night
and listen
to the single, simple cricket
being silent as a monk.

When my silence grows less noisy,
when, like the cricket,
I can pray,
then I will be a spider
leaving
this silky, sticky net of poetry
joining the raindrops
in their freefall
joyfully
trusting.

I will land among the
landless
Tibetans in their robes
who dreamt they were driven out

by a militant equality—
and then awoke.

With them I will believe
in goats and rivers,
and know that in the moonlight
none are homeless.

I will fall further with the rivers,
cast rainbows at the
edge of the precipice,
plunge dancing to the depth
of the abyss.

I will dream deeper with
the goats, live the fifth incarnation
of clover and grass.

Guiltless,
I will imbibe the night,
become drunk on the wind,
suddenly recognize that
round, white moon
as the empty bottom
of my upturned glass.

In the morning I will spy my last
penny, the sun, wedged behind
the lip of the horizon—
it must have fallen from my pocket
last night

as I staggered blissfully
down the road across the sky.

Still drunk on wind and out of
pennies, I'll throw all my tomorrows
into a toboggan, slip
over the edge of the slope, scrape

flying sparks
from the ice in the dark,
crash right into
the Creator—
and slip on through,
licking the frosty taste
of heaven off my lips—

Heaven has *the* best flavor—

No pity at all to it.

From a Northbound Train

Sun setting, seen from
a northbound train:

a radioactive pomegranate,
trimmed smooth—
its lower edge aligned
with the asphalt surface
of a trestle highway
bridging swampland—

rolling along the road,
racing the train for an hour—
a child in red pajamas
gleefully eluding his nurse,
running through the garden,
refusing to be put to bed,
the occasional car
but a nursery toy
left out on the courtyard's
cobblestones.

The Platform

I sit outside the station, waiting
for the train, its long, low call,
its huffing down to slow, its metal-
rails-chalkboard-nails stop.

It is the last train of the afternoon,
people are rushing—and I watch
their shoes, stamping stumbling
tripping laces loose and scurrying

and all aboard, the doors all sealed,
chunk and grind and I'm waiting
for the train, the very last rumble-
shrieking car to slide on past

along the flesh-ferrying track.
When it's gone, there's quiet
for a bit and pigeons come
to where I sit, each pecking about

and checking out the scene, pigeons
on the platform, snatching beaks
and scratching feet, they glean
where commuters missed the trash.

I sit outside the station, waiting
for the setting sun, and when the evening
takes the sun to bed, I wait for the birds
to leave, reach in my pocket,

open the outside locker
with my keys, and from that room
get out the broom and sweep.

ACKNOWLEDGMENTS

I would like to thank the editors of the organizations, print publications and websites where the following poems first appeared, some in previous versions:

Conclave: A Journal of Character #6
My Grandfather's Parka, Slow-Winning: Peace Lesson From Smith and White, My Grandfather's Parka

RiverLit - 100 Words
Mary Martha, Ogham: How the Rain Writes 'Forever'

RiverLit - Bones
Catching the Eye of al-Samakah

Theodate - Ekphrasis
Tea with Josiah II

The Dead Mule School of Southern Literature
Disability and Dog

Tupelo Press 30/30 Project (January 2014)
Offering, Returning from Machu Picchu, Miss Caroline Pickersgill Remembers, Hush, It's a PIRATE!, Meditatio Divina, Fable One: Separation, Fable Two: Climbing, Fable Three: Pausing, Fable Four: Rooting and Rotting, Fable Five: Immersion, Fable Six: Dance, Fable Seven: Destruction, Fable Eight: Grafting, Fable Nine: Gathering, Fable Ten/The End: Greeting, Almost Seven, Pas de Deux - Choreographed by Clark's Grebes, Version, Weeping Birch, Call It a Win

ADDITIONAL THANKS

Savannah Thorne at Balkan Press and Dale Wisely at Ambidextrous Bloodhound (Right Hand Pointing / One Sentence Poems / White Knuckle Chaps);

Jose Angel Araguz and William Bernhardt for reading my pre-publication poetry manuscripts (*last penny the sun* and *Returning to Awe* respectively) and permitting me to use their kind words in print;

Desert Moon Review poetry workshop; Tupelo Press editors Kirsten Miles, Jeffrey Levine, and Marie Gauthier; Tupelo Press 30/30 project team-mates and alumni;

My husband Kevin Kaminski, my mother Joyce Mathison, and all the individuals mentioned in the dedications of these poems, both those who have gone before and those still present;

Highway, the shelter-rescue dog who has taught me so much about becoming a more fully human being; and

Sean Dustman, Ash Bowen, and Ayla Yeargain. Because.

Finally, a most humble thanks to each of you, my readers. I am sincerely grateful for your continued company on this journey, and for all the wonderful comments, emails and letters I've received from you. For those who don't already have my email address, feel free to use the "Contact Me" form on my online poetry page "The Ark of Identity" (arkofidentity.wordpress.com).

All the best to each of you. I wish you peace.

COVER PHOTO

"Sun Shot" photograph by Madeline Kaminski, used with permission. Anyone interested in purchasing fine art prints of "Sun Shot" or other photographs by Madeline Kaminski may use the "Contact Me" form on the author's webpage to request additional information. (arkofidentity.wordpress.com)

ABOUT THE AUTHOR

Laura M Kaminski lives on Carver Creek in Iron County, Missouri with her husband Kevin. Her poetry has been published or is forthcoming in Conclave: A Journal of Character, RiverLit, Kansas City Voices, Right Hand Pointing, VietNow, One Sentence Poems, the 'Ekphrasis' sections of Theodate, the Tupelo Press 30/30 project (January 2014), The First Day, and elsewhere, including the *Homeland: Writings About Homelessness* Good Works charity fundraiser anthology forthcoming from FutureCycle Press in 2014. She has also recently joined the editorial team at Ambidextrous Bloodhound / Right Hand Pointing to help with special projects.

Her poetry chapbook *Returning to Awe* is available from Amazon, and links to her poetry online are posted on her poetry practice blog "The Ark of Identity" at arkofidentity.wordpress.com. Readers are welcome to reach her with comments using the "Contact Me" form on "The Ark of Identity" blog page.